Electricity

Anna Claybourne

First published in the UK in 2016 by
QED Publishing
Part of The Quarto Group
The Old Brewery, 6 Blundell Street,
London, N7 9BH

A catalogue record for this book is available from the British Library.

ISBN 978 1 78493 523 8

Printed and bound in China

Publisher: Maxime Boucknooghe
Editorial Director: Victoria Garrard
Art Director: Miranda Snow
Series Editor: Claudia Martin
Series Designer: Bruce Marshall
Photographer: Michael Wicks
Illustrator: John Haslam
Consultant: Penny Johnson

Words in **bold** can be found in the glossary on page 22.

CONTENTS

3

Electric world

Most of us use electrical things every day. What can you see around you that runs on electricity?

We use electic lights in our houses. Street lamps and traffic lights are also electric.

Radios and televisions run on electricity. You might play with electric toys and video games, too.

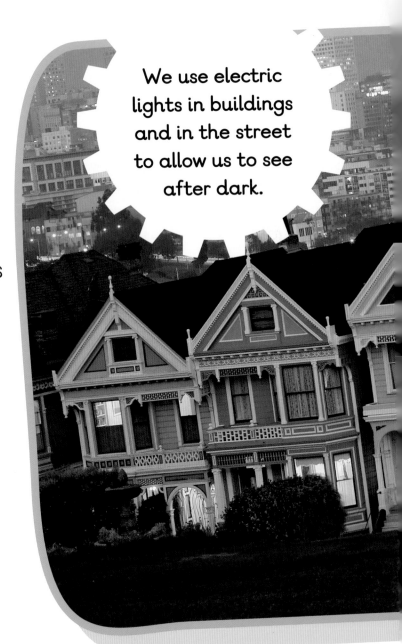

We use electric lights in buildings and in the street to allow us to see after dark.

Electricity makes our lives easier. There are electric trains, cars and buses and we use electric telephones.

Electrical **appliances** make cooking and cleaning quicker and easier.

WARNING!
Never play with electrical devices or **sockets**. The electricity supply can be very dangerous.

What does electricity do?

Energy is needed to make things work and electricity is a type of energy. Electrical appliances turn electricity into other kinds of energy, such as heat, sound, light or movement.

Blender

Iron

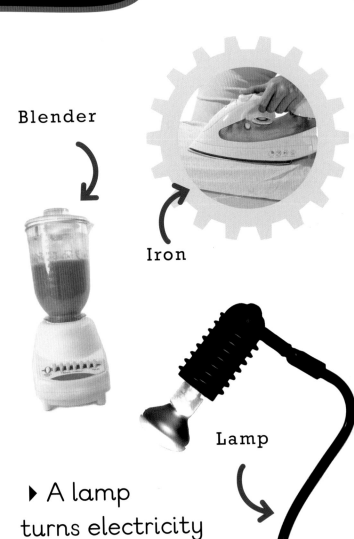

Lamp

▸ A lamp turns electricity into light.

Television

Tablets

Toaster

▶ A toaster turns electricity into heat to toast bread.

▶ An electric fan has a blade that spins round very fast to make a breeze.

Fan

▼ A hairdryer turns electricity into heat, sound and movement.

Hairdryer

Plugged in!

Electric current is electricity that comes from a power station. When applicances in your house plug into walls, the electric current passes in through wires.

TRY THIS

Make a list of electrical appliances that you have around your home. Do you use all the things pictured here?

Where does electricity come from?

Most of the electricity we use is made at big buildings called power stations.

Electricity travels along thick wires from the power station. These wires hang on tall towers called pylons. Thinner wires take the electricity to the sockets in our homes.

Pylons carry electricity along thick wires to our homes.

We plug appliances, such as toasters and lamps, into sockets to connect them to the electricity supply.

Some power stations use energy stored in coal, oil or gas to make electricity. Electricity can also come from other forms of energy, such as the wind, the sun, or moving water.

This power station turns energy from moving water into electricity.

A wind **turbine** turns energy from the wind into electricity.

Making a circuit

An electrical circuit is a loop that electricity can flow around. You can make your own using sticky tape, a battery, two pieces of electrical wire, a small bulb and a bulb holder. Buy them from a hardware shop.

Electrical wires are usually made of a metal called copper, which is coated with plastic. Ask an adult to cut the plastic layer off the ends of each wire.

Terminals

9-volt battery

200mAh

A 9-volt battery is the simplest to use. All batteries have two **terminals**.

Plastic coating

Copper wire

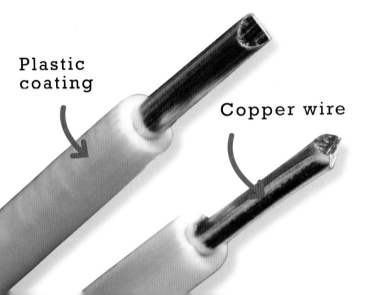

Make sure each wire only touches one terminal.

TRY THIS

1 Twist the bare end of one wire around a battery terminal. Fix it in place with sticky tape.

2 Fix the other wire to the second terminal in the same way, using sticky tape.

3 Carefully screw the bulb into the inside of the bulb holder.

4 Take the two free ends of the wires. Touch them to the two **contacts** of the bulb holder. Your bulb should glow!

Contact

Contact

Bulb holder

Electric light

How does a light bulb work? You can find out by taking a closer look at your circuit.

Bulb

The wires in your circuit link one terminal of the battery to the other. This makes a loop that electricity from the battery can flow around.

The electricity travels through the light bulb. A bulb has a very thin wire inside of it, called a filament. When electricity passes through the filament, it makes it get hot and glow.

Filament

It's a fact!
The more batteries you add to your circuit, the brighter the bulb will glow.

Better bulbs

Many people use low-energy light bulbs in their homes. These bulbs use less electricity than ordinary light bulbs. Ordinary bulbs waste a lot of electricity by turning it into heat. Low-energy bulbs stay cooler!

Your bulb is turning electricity into light and heat.

Light loops

Electric lights in your house work on a circuit, just like the one you made. Electricity flows around the circuit, and through the bulb.

13

Switching on and off

You use a switch to turn most electrical appliances on and off.

To turn the appliance on, the switch connects the wires together to form a full circuit.

Electricity flows around and makes the appliance work. You can see this idea in action in your circuit.

Wire

Contact

TRY THIS

Switch the light bulb on by touching the wire to the contact.

When you move the wire away, you break the loop. The light goes out. The bulb is off.

You press a switch to turn a hairdryer on and off. Pressing the switch off breaks the circuit. Pressing the switch on connects the wires again.

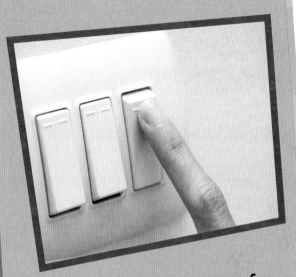

A light switch is part of a big circuit inside the walls of a building. It makes a loop linking the light to the electricity supply.

WARNING!

Never touch electrical switches with wet hands. Electricity can flow through water and give you a very harmful electric shock.

Static electricity

Static electricity is a different kind of electricity. Unlike electric current, which flows through wires, static electricity collects in an object, such as a comb.

Comb

TRY THIS

You will need a plastic comb or pen, a woolly jumper and some tissue paper.

1 Tear off a few small pieces of tissue paper and put them on a table.

2 Rub the comb (or a pen) firmly on the jumper. Hold the comb close to the tissue paper.

Jumper

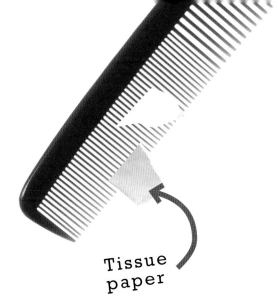

Tissue paper

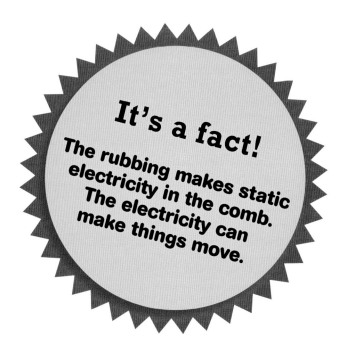

3 The comb should attract the bits of tissue paper towards it. (If it doesn't, try rubbing the comb on the jumper for longer.)

Electric amber

Long ago, an ancient Greek found that if he rubbed **amber** on cat fur, the amber would pull tiny objects towards it.

Amber

▶ Static electricity can build up in many objects.

Electric hair

Static electricity will make your hair stand on end!

TRY THIS

To make your hair electric, all you need is a balloon.

1 Ask an adult to blow up the balloon and tie the end. This works best if the balloon is full of air.

2 Rub the balloon quickly on your hair. The cleaner you hair is, the better this will work.

3 The quick rubbing movement makes static electricity collect in your hair. Your hair will start to stick up in all directions!

Sometimes pulling off a woolly hat can make your hair electric too!

It's a fact!
As all the hairs become electric, they push away from each other. This makes them stand up and away from your head in different directions.

Spark in the dark

Static electricity can jump across a gap, making a visable spark. See for yourself with this experiment.

TRY THIS

You need a plastic comb or pen, and a woolly jumper.

1 Rub the comb hard and fast on a jumper to build up a lot of static electricity in the comb.

2 Hold the comb as close to a radiator or a metal sink tap as you can without touching.

Jumper

Comb

Supermarket shock

Static electricity can build up in supermarket trolleys. When you touch them, the electricity can jump into you and give you a fright.

3 A small spark should jump across the gap between the comb and the metal. If you do the experiment in the dark, you will be more likely see it.

You might hear a tiny 'click' when the spark jumps.

Be careful not to bump into things if you do this experiment in the dark!

GLOSSARY

Amber
Resin that has hardened over millions of years. Resin is sticky and oozes from trees.

Appliance
A useful machine, such as a kettle. Electrical appliances run on electricity.

Battery
A container that stores electrical energy. When a battery is connected to a circuit, it makes electricity flow.

Contacts
Metal parts of a bulb, or other object, that can be connected to an electric circuit.

Electric current
A flow of electricity through a wire or other substance.

Energy
The power to make things work, happen or move.

Socket
A device on a wall, through which you can connect an appliance to the electricity supply.

Static electricity
Electricity that builds up in an object, and does not flow.

Switch
A gap in a circuit. It can be closed to let electricity flow, or opened to stop the flow.

Terminals
Metal parts of a battery that can be connected to an electric circuit.

Turbine
A machine used in producing electricity. A turbine has blades that are turned by wind, steam or water.

INDEX

NEXT STEPS

※ Experiments in this book use small batteries and small amounts of electricity that cannot give dangerous electric shocks. However, children must be reminded that electricity can be dangerous and harmful. Make sure they know not to play with electric items, and not to touch them with wet hands.

※ Try counting all the electric lights inside your house or school, including small on/off lights and indicator lights on appliances.

※ Lightning is a giant spark of static electricity. If you can do so safely, let children watch electrical storms with you and look out for lightning sparks. Talk about how lightning builds up in clouds, then jumps across the gap between the clouds and the ground.

※ Let children watch you open up an electrical device such as a computer (only do this if it is safe to do so according to the manufacturer). Show them the wires inside the machine while explaining that electricity runs through the wires to make the machine work.

※ Look out for electrical circuits and switches inside and out. Talk about how they might work. Examples include the button you press to stop traffic at a pedestrian crossing, strings of Christmas lights, and the light that turns on in the refrigerator when you open the door.

※ Point out overhead cables and pylons carrying electricity to different buildings. Talk about where electricity comes from. It can be made by burning coal or oil in power stations, or from wind or water turning turbines.